Costa del Sol
Travel Guide

Quick Trips Series

No part of this publication may be reproduced, stored in a retrieval system, or transmitted, in any form or by any means without the prior written permission of the publisher, nor be otherwise circulated in any form of binding or cover other than that in which it is published and without similar condition being imposed on the subsequent purchaser. If there are any errors or omissions in copyright acknowledgements the publisher will be pleased to insert the appropriate acknowledgement in any subsequent printing of this publication. Although we have taken all reasonable care in researching this book we make no warranty about the accuracy or completeness of its content and disclaim all liability arising from its use.

Copyright © 2016, Astute Press
All Rights Reserved.

Table of Contents

COSTA DEL SOL   6
- 🌐 CUSTOMS & CULTURE 9
- 🌐 GEOGRAPHY 11
- 🌐 WEATHER & BEST TIME TO VISIT 12

SIGHTS & ACTIVITIES: WHAT TO SEE & DO   15
- 🌐 MARBELLA 15
- 🌐 PUERTO BANÚS 17
- 🌐 NIGHT CLUBS & CELEBRITY SPOTTING IN MARBELLA 20
  - Olivia Valere 20
- 🌐 ESTEPONA 21
  - Selwo Aventura 22
  - Palaeontology Museum of Estepona 23
- 🌐 FUENGIROLA 24
  - Castle of Sohail 25
  - Bioparc Fuengirola 26
- 🌐 BENALMADENA 26
  - Butterfly Park 27
  - Jardin de las Aguilas 28
- 🌐 MIJAS 29
  - Virgen de la Peña 29
  - Museum of Miniatures 30
  - Mayan Monkey Mijas 31
- 🌐 NERJA 31

Donkey Sanctuary...33
Nerja Caves...34
🌐 Malaga..35
Alcazaba 36
Museo Automovilistico De Malaga.....................................36
Dolls House Museum 38
Picasso Museum 39
🌐 Day Trip To Gibraltar 40

BUDGET TIPS   42

🌐 Accommodation 42
Hotel Molina Lario..42
Suite Novotel Malaga Centro 43
Hotel Isabelle, Torremolinos 44
Hotel Casa Rosa...45
La Villa Marbella...45
🌐 Places to Eat 46
The Lounge at Pinoccios, Benalmadena...............................46
Tapeo de Cervantes, Malaga..47
Samsara Deli Café, Mijas 48
El Gato Lounge, Torremolinos 49
La Plaza, Malaga 50
🌐 Shopping 51
Artesania de Espana, Mijas..51
Costa del Sol Markets..51
Tickled Pink, Mijas Pueblo..53
Old Town, Marbella...53
Shopping Malls..54

KNOW BEFORE YOU GO   55

🌐 Entry Requirements 55
🌐 Health Insurance...55
🌐 Travelling with Pets 56

- 🌐 AIRPORTS 57
- 🌐 AIRLINES 58
- 🌐 CURRENCY 59
- 🌐 BANKING & ATMS 59
- 🌐 CREDIT CARDS 59
- 🌐 TOURIST TAXES 60
- 🌐 RECLAIMING VAT 60
- 🌐 TIPPING POLICY 61
- 🌐 MOBILE PHONES 61
- 🌐 DIALLING CODE 62
- 🌐 EMERGENCY NUMBERS 63
- 🌐 PUBLIC HOLIDAYS 63
- 🌐 TIME ZONE 64
- 🌐 DAYLIGHT SAVINGS TIME 64
- 🌐 SCHOOL HOLIDAYS 65
- 🌐 TRADING HOURS 65
- 🌐 DRIVING LAWS 65
- 🌐 DRINKING LAWS 66
- 🌐 SMOKING LAWS 66
- 🌐 ELECTRICITY 67
- 🌐 FOOD & DRINK 67

COSTA DEL SOL TRAVEL GUIDE

Costa del Sol

With its pleasant climate and proximity to northern Europe, the Costa del Sol has been attracting tourists for centuries. The famous resort cities of Marbella, Puerto Banus, Torremolinos and Benalmadena are quick and cheap airline flights away from the colder European winters.

COSTA DEL SOL TRAVEL GUIDE

Often regarded as the "California of Europe" this region can be relied upon for plentiful sunshine, beautiful scenery, golf courses to satisfy all and interesting pockets of Spanish culture.

Mediterranean cruise ships pass here and proximity to North Africa and the Strait of Gibraltar, also makes the Costa del Sol a convenient base from which to set off on a short excursion to Morocco.

Malaga, the capital of the Costa del Sol, is associated with one of the most famous modern artists of all - Pablo Picasso, the father of Cubism. Another famous son of the region is the actor Antonio Banderas, who was perhaps best known for his role as the masked Zorro. Banderas was born in Malaga.

COSTA DEL SOL TRAVEL GUIDE

Despite its popularity with tourists, the city of Malaga also offers a robust business location with suitable venues for hosting regular trade fairs and expos. It is the fourth largest city in Spain. The tourist industry, however, is centered in other locations, most notably the popular and affluent Marbella. Malaga is a modern city with well over half a million inhabitants.

Different sections of the Costa del Sol appeal to different types of visitors. While Marbella attracts the affluent, the trendy and the high-profile glitterati, Benalmadena and Fuengirola is more suited to family entertainment and Torremolinos has emerged as a region more tolerant to gay and lesbian visitors than most other parts of Spain.

In some regions, such as Torrox and Torre del Mar, the rapid speed at which the tourist boom of the 1960s and

COSTA DEL SOL TRAVEL GUIDE

1970s took off, led to large walls of high-rise apartment and holiday buildings. In others, the Andalucian village charm has been preserved.

Some of the settlements that grew into towns and cities around the Costa del Sol date back to the 8th century BC. The fertile coast was first colonized by the sea faring Phoenicians, and has since seen the likes of successions of Carthaginians, Romans, Visigoths, Vandals and Moors.

Casares is famous for a healing spa where Julius Caesar allegedly sought healing for a liver complaint. It was in this region that the Moorish influence in Spain lingered the longest, leaving behind a series of Forts and remnants of old mosques. With the Reconquesta, a new era of Catholic revival followed.

COSTA DEL SOL TRAVEL GUIDE

Many churches and other religious shrines date back to this era, that was characterized by many visions of the Virgin Mary appearing to religious folk, but also to ordinary inhabitants. After the Civil War, the allure of the region inspired a new generation, leading to its current dominance as a tourist destination.

🌐 Customs & Culture

Although the original inhabitants of the Costa del Sol were Spanish, its popularity as a tourist location and playground for the rich and famous has given it a cosmopolitan flavour.

Between 10 and 15 percent of its residents are foreign born. At the resorts you will find that many of the workers are fluent in languages such as English, French, German, Japanese and Norwegian.

COSTA DEL SOL TRAVEL GUIDE

Local Spanish culture to experience includes bullrings, flamenco dancing and the distinctive Spanish guitar melodies. In the spring and summer months the area hosts a variety of festivals, fairs, religious events and celebrations. Art and crafts can be admired or purchased in shops or during the weekly markets at many of the tourist resorts. The area is known for the quality of its ceramics.

You will find many Spaniards welcoming as well as effusive and expressive. The Catholic church dominates religious matters – with many shops closed on Sundays. The cuisine of the area is Spanish and Mediterranean, with extensive international influences.

COSTA DEL SOL TRAVEL GUIDE

There are many elements of the Moorish past on display and hints of Roman influences to be found in the architecture of the Costa del Sol.

🌍 Geography

The Costa del Sol is located along the 150 km strip of land between the Costa Tropical, (also known as Costa de Granada or Costa Granadina) and the Costa de la Luz (with Gibraltar) along the southern coast of Spain. It corresponds roughly to the coastline of the Malaga province, of which the city of Malaga is the capital. Its boundaries are usually regarded as Malaga (or the beautiful Nerja) on the eastern side and Marbella/Estepona to the west.

Once only a collection of humble fishing villages, the activities of several high-profile developers have

COSTA DEL SOL TRAVEL GUIDE

transformed it to one of the most popular tourist destinations in Europe.

As a cruise location in the Mediterranean, The Costa del Sol can also be reached by sea, whether by luxury cruise liner or aboard your own yacht. The Costa del Sol has 11 marinas and around 4500 moorings to accommodate private vessels.

Pablo Ruiz Picasso Airport, just outside Malaga, connects to various other locations in Spain, Europe and other cities around the world. There is a bus service from the airport. Frequent bus and rail services are operated between the towns and cities of Costa del Sol.

There are several bus companies that operate in and around the Costa del Sol, including the Eurolines service

COSTA DEL SOL TRAVEL GUIDE

that links Malaga, to locations such as Belgium, Portugal, France, Switzerland, Ukraine, Bulgaria, Italy and Morocco.

🌐 Weather & Best Time to Visit

The name Costa del Sol means 'Coast of the Sun'. Areas such as Puerto Banús are warmer as it enjoys the shelter of nearby the northern mountain ranges. The region enjoys a lengthy tourist season from March to November.

Marbella experiences maximum temperatures of 30 degrees Celsius in the high summer months of July and August, and summer lasts from May to September. Even in winter, mountain ranges to the north provide many warmer days.

COSTA DEL SOL TRAVEL GUIDE

From December to February, the maximum temperature averages 17 degrees Celsius and seldom drops below fifteen degrees. Rain does occur, but infrequently. Snow is sometimes visible on nearby mountains, but seldom lasts longer than a day or two. Spring and autumn see temperatures averages between the high teens and the low to mid-twenties, with cooling winds.

In Malaga, to the east, winter temperatures range between 8 and 17 degrees Celsius, while the summer temperatures ranges between 26 and 35 degrees Celsius.

COSTA DEL SOL TRAVEL GUIDE

COSTA DEL SOL TRAVEL GUIDE

Sights & Activities: What to See & Do

🌍 Marbella

With endless stretches of beach running parallel to rows of luxury villas (some of them owned by celebrities), Marbella can be thought of as the Costa del Sol version of France's St Tropez or California's Malibu.

Stars like Bruce Willis, Naomi Campbell, Kate Moss, David and Victoria Beckham and Britney Spears have been spotted here. Antonio Banderas, who was born in nearby Malaga, owns a home in Marbella. Another famous resident is the elusive Korean pop singer Kimera.

Probably one of the wealthiest homeowners in the area had been King Fahd of Saudi Arabia. His palace was a replica of the White House in gold and marble, but the

COSTA DEL SOL TRAVEL GUIDE

property also included two mosques, a hospital, several swimming pools and adjoining villas.

A battalion of personal vehicles ranging from helicopters to luxury cars and a $1 million yacht in the marina had left no one in doubt as to his residency in the summer months. Not only did his presence contribute considerably to the local economy, but he was also a high profile contributor to charitable projects in the area.

Although now very much a retreat of the rich and famous with its Golden Mile, the town had, in the 19th century been a major source of iron, with several high-producing mines accounting for its main economic activity. Orange Square or Plaza de los Naranjos, with its numerous fruit-bearing orange trees show another product of the region - citrus fruit.

COSTA DEL SOL TRAVEL GUIDE

The Old Quarter contains many clues to its rich heritage. The Iglesia Mayor de la Encarnacion on Plaza de la Iglesia, a Catholic church dates back to the 1500s, although its current facade is from 1756. Its interior contains beautiful artwork and some of its icons form part of the processions during Holy Week. It had been one of the last towns to be surrendered by the Moors.

Marbella's fortune changed by chance, when a stopover by Prince Alfonso de Hohenlohe-Langenburg led to his initial investment in the area, a ruined vineyard. In 1954, he opened the Marbella Club Hotel and began inviting his titled friends and acquaintances to the region. Prosperity soon followed.

COSTA DEL SOL TRAVEL GUIDE

🌐 Puerto Banús

Puerto Banús (located very close to Marbella) is often regarded as the trendiest marina in Europe, the port where fame and fortune rub shoulders on a regular basis. The area is named after José Banús, the Marbella property developer who conceived the marina development in the late 1960s. Creative guidance for the project came from Noldi Schrek, an influential Russian-born architect whose work had already left its mark on Beverley Hills and Mexico.

The development was prestigious from its opening in 1970, which was attended by guests such as the Aga Khan, Prince Rainer, Princess Grace, Roman Polanski and Hugh Hefner. A young Julio Iglesias sang at the gala event. The high profile status continued.

COSTA DEL SOL TRAVEL GUIDE

The marine has space to berth 900 vessels and showcases yachts by some of the wealthiest individuals on earth, including Arab royalty and Hollywood actors. It is a great place for spotting celebrities and their luxury toys.

Automobile enthusiasts may glimpse exclusive sport cars here – some of which are not commercially available. Top fashion designers have flagship shops in the streets next to the marina and offer their exclusive lines. Conversely there are some good shops inside the marina offering quality, discounted goods. Aim for Sinatra's famous restaurant and they are nearby.

The bay provides a brilliant view of the 1200m expanse of La Concha mountain. Its name means 'the shell' in Spanish and this distinctive peak forms part of the Sierra Blanca mountain range. Its rugged incline allow various

COSTA DEL SOL TRAVEL GUIDE

interesting hiking possibilities to the summit, although some might not be suitable for novice climbers. There are several simpler walks, with the easiest being the 500m route to Mirador del Corzo. Januar Mountain peak also offers a great scenic vantage point for looking down on Puerto Banús.

Two massive sculptures are recent additions to the marina. One is a sculpture of a rhinocerous in lace by Salvador Dalí, which weighs over three tons. The work, entitled 'Rinoceronte vestido con puntillas', was created in 1956, but only came to its current location in 2004. A 26 m statue by Zurab Tsereteli in bronze and copper, had been a gift of goodwill from the mayor of Moscow. It is entitled 'La Victoria'.

COSTA DEL SOL TRAVEL GUIDE

Boulevard de la Fama de Puerto Banús, or the Boulevard of Fame can be compared to Hollywood's Sunset Boulevard, where stars are awarded to the rich and famous, for eample, Antonio Banderas and Julio Iglesias who contributed to the prestige of the area. For his efforts, the architect Noldi Schrek posthumously received a star in 2010. The Boulevard is lined by small stalls selling mostly antiques.

The area sees five million visitors annually.

🌐 Night Clubs & Celebrity Spotting in Marbella

Olivia Valere

Carretera Istán, KM 0,800 29600 Marbella

Tel: 952 828 861

http://www.ang.oliviavaleremarbella.es

COSTA DEL SOL TRAVEL GUIDE

A popular night-time venue frequented by the rich and famous is Olivia Valere, named after its charismatic owner. After successfully running a discoteque called "Apocalipse" in Paris for several years, a chance encounter involving the operatic pop singer Kimera led to a new business venture in Marbella.

The interior of the club is styled to resemble an Arabian fantasy, including stately olive trees, the allure of candles and the exquisite fragrance of orange blossom. The dining menu features a variety of inventive international dishes.

Another great nightspot for a spell of people watching is Sinatras (at the Puerto Banus Marina). It is a frequent

COSTA DEL SOL TRAVEL GUIDE

haunt of Hollywood actors, supermodels and sport celebs but the drinks are affordable and service is quite swift.

🌏 Estepona

While Estepona might not offer the same nightlife or power-shopping opportunities as some of the more popular tourist spots on the Costa del Sol, it does make up for it in authentic Spanish charm.

The sunny climate and its quieter beaches makes Estepona a popular choice. El Christo beach, with its fine sand, and pristine, shallow water carries blue flag status and is pleasantly sheltered from the wind.

Some of the sights of the town include the Torre Reloj or the clock tower and the Church of Los Remedios, which dates back to the 1700s and had once been a Franciscan monastry.

The town has an old bull ring and a museum dedicated to the culture of bull-fighting. The daily fish market is another sight to behold, but you need to be an early bird to observe its most characteristic interactions.

Selwo Aventura

Autovia Costa del Sol Km 162. 5, Estepona

Tel: 902 19 04 82

http://www.selwo.es/

One unusual attraction near Estepona is the Selwo Aventura, a game park with a collection of over 2000 rare animals representing different continents that can be observed in their natural state on safari-like tours.

COSTA DEL SOL TRAVEL GUIDE

This can be done from a truck or the back of a camel.

The complex includes sections such as Lion Hill, Tiger Gorge, the Ravine of the Bears, but also a garden aviary and a petting zoo for the kids. Some of the other animals include rhinos, giraffes, zebras, monkeys, buffalo and alligators. Another awe-inspiring route takes you along three suspended bridges.

Admission is 24,50€ per adult.

Palaeontology Museum of Estepona

Plaza de Toros, Estepona

Tel: 280 57 09

http://www.infoestepona.com/museos/paleontologico.sht

COSTA DEL SOL TRAVEL GUIDE

ml

The Palaeontology museum has an extensive collection of about 2000 fossils dating back to the Pliocene Period of about four million years ago. The Estepona Basil has yielded rich finds from this epoch in fauna and flora, including around 600 different species. The display also includes replicas of Argentinean dinosaurs. Inquire with the guides about the possibility of viewing the Dolmen of Corominas.

🌐 Fuengirola

Once a modest fishing village, Fuengirola has developed noticably with the influx of tourism to the Costa del Sol. Today it is popular with a mostly British crowd looking for good value, family holidays in the sun. Popular are British pubs, English breakfasts, Premier League football on Sky

COSTA DEL SOL TRAVEL GUIDE

Sports TV channels and music entertainment in local establishments every evening.

The Paseo Maritimo, a 7 km boardwalk hugging the coastline of Fuengirola, provides a pleasant scenic stroll, by day or by night, and its beaches provide a pleasant setting for sunbathing or diving.

The town has a bullring (Plaza de Toros), if you wish to explore that side of Spanish culture. There are also ruins from Roman times nearby. Visit the Fuengirola street market when hunting for authentic souvenirs such as pottery and handicrafts.

Castle of Sohail

A7 Motorway, Fuengirola

COSTA DEL SOL TRAVEL GUIDE

Located near the mouth of the Fuengirola River, the castle of Sohail provides an excellent vantage point for strategic observation. It has a long history, dating back to the crude structures of early Punic inhabitants. King Abdderraman III built a modest fort in the 10th century, which was expanded upon in the 12th century by the Almoravides.

The hilltop fortification of Castle Sohail was occupied in 1485 by Christian resistance to the Nazari forces of Granada. Various occupants brought modifications. An earlier gate in the north was changed and an eastern tower was sacrificed for an area to accommodate cannons. Stables were added to house a cavalry unit.

After decades of decline, a restoration project began in 1989. It has been used as a venue for special celebrations, concerts and festivals.

Bioparc Fuengirola

Avenida Camilo Jose Cela 8-10, 29640 Fuengirola

Tel: 952 666 301

http://www.zoofuengirola.com

Making excellent use of all available space, the zoo at Fuengirola uses the creative placement of plant cover and glass to create displays that seem as natural and unobtrusive as possible. As the zoo is open by night as well, it provides a great opportunity to observe the more elusive nocturnal birds and animals.

Benalmadena

Despite rapid expansions on the outer regions of town to accommodate the 100,000 visitors Benalmadena sees each summer, its historical heart has retained much of the original charm and character.

Although the town hosts a vibrant night life, it also has a number of family-friendly attractions nearby, such as the amusement park at Tivoli World, a mini golf course, an aquarium that included a special "penguinarium" to accommodate the Antarctic birds, a Buddhist temple and the opportunity to view a demonstration in Spanish Dressage at Club El Ranchito, for the rather steep price of 77 €.

The long beach promenade features the display of a variety of mosaics in different and divergent styles, all by local artists. The beachfront also offers a large selection of local restaurants.

Butterfly Park

Calle Muerdago, s/n (Beside Buddhist Temple), 29639 Benalmadena

Tel: 951 211 196

http://www.mariposariodebenalmadena.com/English/index.html

Butterfly Park contains specimens from the Philippines, Belize, Kenya, Malaysia and Costa Rica. There are over a 150 separate species and care has been taken to incorporate indigenous plants from their country of origin. Besides the butterflies, the facility also has squirrels, birds and even iguanas.

COSTA DEL SOL TRAVEL GUIDE

Jardin de las Aguilas

Next to Castillo de Colomares

Tel : 952 568 239

Jardin de las Aguilas (Garden of the Eagles) offers visitors the opportunity to experience the beauty and skills of around 160 birds of prey, ranging from eagles, falcons, hawks, condors and vultures. There are daily shows in the holiday season. Admission is 6€ for adults. Other nearby attractions includes the Castillo de Colomares, a recent, but beautiful monument to Christopher Columbus and Snake City, a facility with a collection of snakes and other reptiles.

Mijas

Mijas had been populated from Roman times, when it had been a trading post between Malaga and Cadiz. Only ruins remain of the Moorish castle, but there are a number of other areas of interest in this affluent hilltop and coastal town.

The old village, Mijas Pueblo overlooks the Mediterranean coast from a height of 428 m and displays the usual Andalucian setting of distinctively white structures separated by narrow cobbled streets. The newer parts of Mijas are rapidly becoming integrated with its neighbor Fuengirola. The town has a variety of picturesque spring and summer celebrations and festivals.

Virgen de la Peña

Paseo "The Compass"

Virgen de la Peña is an image of the Holy Virgin Mary that was discovered in a cave shrine in 1586, by two children of the village after a mystical vision. Allegedly it had remained hidden during the centuries of Moorish occupation. It can be viewed free of charge. On Wednesdays at noon, this is the setting of a free flamenco performance.

Museum of Miniatures

Avda Compass, s / n. 29650 Mijas.

Tel: 952 58 90 34

For the most eccentric collection of items, the displays of Juan Millan (a stage hypnotist better known as Professor Max) must be seen to be believed. The essence of many of the objects can only be appreciated with the aid of strong magnifying glasses.

See an intricate ballerina carved from a toothpick, a portrait of Leonardo da Vinci on a grain of rice and a portrait of Abraham Lincoln painted on a pin's head.

The most grisly display is no doubt that of an authentically shrunk head of a white missionary, allegedly acquired in person from a tribe in Africa. Entrance is 3€.

Mayan Monkey Mijas

524 Plaza de Constitucion, 29650 Mijas

Tour the mini chocolate factory at Mayan Monkey Mijas to see how chocolate is made, or perhaps and, if you like, try your hand at making some yourself.

COSTA DEL SOL TRAVEL GUIDE

 Nerja

Perched at the edge of spectacular cliffs and characterized by white Mediterranean housing and narrow cobbled streets, Nerja embodies the romantic image of Andalucia's yesterdays. Several coves along the coast of Nerja provide ideal opportunities for Scuba diving. Nearby mountain ranges, such as Sierra de Burno, Sierra Tejeda and Sierra de Almijara provide majestic scenery.

A breathtaking view can be obtained from the Balcón de Europa, a fort located on a rocky outcrop. Once a necessary defence point against English pirates, the fort and its surroundings now form part of a promenade which sees plenty of footfall by day and by night. Across from the castle, you can visit the 16th century Church of El Salvador, which features some beautiful interior artwork.

COSTA DEL SOL TRAVEL GUIDE

The Balcón de Europa now hosts a restaurant known as Plaza Balcón de Europa.

On the balcony you will also find the famous statue of King Alfonso XII, who was the first to refer to this place as the Balcony of Europe.

The Natural Park of Maro or Cerro Gordo offers an unspoilt stretch of land with a great selection of natural plant and animal life. Along the road from Nerja to Maro, you can enjoy the impressive sight of the El Aguila Aqueduct, a 19th century construction built to facilitate the movement of water from a spring in Maro to the San Joaquín de Maro sugar factory.

Nerja is on the south coast about one hour's drive away from Granada (which is to the north and is the last

Moorish outpost in Spain). Nerja is about 45 minutes drive to the east of Malaga.

A bus route links Nerja to Malaga, Granada, Seville, Torre del Mar and several other locations.

Donkey Sanctuary

N - 340 Coast Road, 29780, Nerja

34 66 455 8133

http://www.nerjadonkeysanctuary.com

Another attraction near to Nerja is its donkey sanctuary. You could just pay a visit and, purchase a bucket of carrots and other treats for 2€ and pass them to these amiable creatures, but there is also the option to get involved with their "voluntourism" programme. Besides donkeys, there are also sheep, horses and pigs. The donkey sanctuary is part of the WWOOF programme (http://ruralvolunteers.org) that sets up visiting volunteers with rural hosts.

Nerja Caves

http://www.thenerjacaves.com/

The Nerja Caves were discovered by five youths in early in 1959 who accessed it through a sinkhole called 'La Mina'. The caves contain the largest stalagmite in the world at 32m tall. There are also columns in a section known as the Organ Corner, which produce different musical pitches when struck. It has been theorized that human intervention may have played a role in this effect.

COSTA DEL SOL TRAVEL GUIDE

There are several different halls within the caverns. The Hall of the Waterfall or Ballet incorporates a natural amphitheatre that can seat 100 persons.

Human remains suggest that the limestone caves had been inhabited from as early as 25,000 BC and excavation has revealed interesting clues about the lifestyle and diet of prehistoric peoples in the form of bone and stone tools, cave paintings and fragments of pottery and textiles. It was still used periodically by humans as recently as 3800 BC. Admission is 7€ for adults.

🌎 Malaga

As the capital of the Costa del Sol region, Malaga is the fourth largest city in Spain, a modern hub of business that is in reality one of the oldest cities in Europe.

COSTA DEL SOL TRAVEL GUIDE

There are two prominent Moorish structures, the Castle of Gibralfaro and the fort at Alcazaba, both dating back to the 11th century. It is also the birthplace of one of the most famous modern artists, Pablo Picasso.

Malaga is often overlooked by tourists who arrive at the airport and immediately head to the Costa del Sol resorts to the west and east. Take some time here. Malaga is a beautiful city, well worth a day trip or an entire city-break holiday.

Alcazaba

Alcazabilla s/n, 29015 Malaga

Tel: 952 217 646

Built on a hill by Badis Ben Habus, the fort of Alcazaba offers a splendid view of Malaga's port. It was constructed in close proximity to the ruins of a Roman theatre from 2nd century BC. It is one of the best preserved examples of a Moorish citadel. While an outer wall was destroyed, the fountains and the gardens remain. The complex is now the location of the Málaga Archaeological Museum.

Museo Automovilistico De Malaga

Avda Sor Teresa Prat, 15, 29003 Malaga

(Formerly Automobile Museum of Malaga)

Tel: 951 13 70 01

http://www.museoautomovilmalaga.com/en/

Malaga's Museo Automovilistico de Malaga was founded by Joao Manuel Magalhaes, originally from Oporto in Portugal, a avid collector of classical automobiles.

COSTA DEL SOL TRAVEL GUIDE

Magalhaes' native country showed no interest in affording official recognition to the formidable collection of 85 vintage cars, but Spain's Ministry of Culture approached several cities about the possibility of hosting a museum and Malaga won the award.

Some of the vehicles on display are true works of art such as the Swarovsky encrusted Rolls Royce from 1985 and the Flower Power Rolls Royce from the sixties.

The oldest vehicle is a stately Winner from the year 1898. Some of the true classics include a 1907 Jackson, a 1907 Richmond, a 1916 Buick, a 1919 Lancia, a 1930 Studebaker, a 1929 Morris Minor and a 1936 Bugatti. There are exotic rarities that never made it onto popular production lines and cars that are celebrated because of famous owners such as Sylvester Stallone or Arnold Schwarzenegger.

You will have the opportunity to experience a close encounter with the Spirit of Ecstacy, the distinctive hood sculpture associated with Rolls Royce. This well-known figure was created by the artist Charles Sykes and modelled on Eleanor Thornton, mistress of the second Baron Montagu of Beaulieu. History buffs might be particularly interested in the Lancia Italia used by Mussolini or Heinrich Himmler's Mercedes 540K. Admission is 6€ for adults.

Dolls House Museum

Calle Alamos, 32, Malaga, Spain

Tel: 952-210-082

http://www.museocm.com/

COSTA DEL SOL TRAVEL GUIDE

The Museum contains an impressive collection of doll's houses, particularly from the 19th century and focusing on Andalusian manufacture. Many of the dolls exhibited are also dressed in traditional Andalusian costume. They have miniature horse carriages outside, or feature miniature guitars or other objects made with exquisite detail. The oldest exhibit, a Majorcan house, dates back to 1850.

Admission is €5 for adults. There is a museum shop that sells miniature furniture, artefacts and collectable dolls. The owner of the museum, Voria Harras, is a multi-skilled restorer of doll houses and her fascination began through an incredible synchronicity when her husband bought her a doll's house as a gift that had once belonged to her own mother.

Picasso Museum

Palacio de Buenavista

C/ San Agustín, 8. 29015 Málaga

Tel: 952 127600

http://www2.museopicassomalaga.org

The first abortive attempt for a museum of Picasso's work in Malaga had come from the artist himself in 1953, but nothing was finalized or achieved.

In the 1990s, the artist's daughter in law, Christine Ruiz-Picasso began the initiative that was to culminate in a museum inaugurated in 2003 by King Juan Carlos I and Queen Sofia. The process of renovations revealed that the 450-year-old building hid a secret - it lay on the ruins of a fish factory dating back to the epoch of the

COSTA DEL SOL TRAVEL GUIDE

Phoenicians.

The large collection of works at the Picasso museum includes drawings, paintings, ceramics, sculptures and illustrations. Nearby, at Plaza de La Merced, is the birthplace of Picasso.

Day Trip To Gibraltar

Gibraltar is located about 45 minutes drive to the west of Marbella. Take your passport as it is a part of the United Kingdom and there is a passport control.

Affectionately known as The Rock, Gibraltar is home to over 500 plant species and a variety of interesting fauna, including the famous wild monkey colony. The 426m high outcrop of Jurassic limestone offers unique views of the Atlantic Ocean and its surroundings. Gibraltar had been

COSTA DEL SOL TRAVEL GUIDE

under British control since 1704 and its residents have actively resisted re-integration into Spain since. It is a haven for tourists seeking tax-free bargains.

COSTA DEL SOL TRAVEL GUIDE

Budget Tips

 Accommodation

Hotel Molina Lario

c/ Molina Lario 20-22, 29015 Malaga

http://www.hotelmolinalario.com/en/

Built from two refurbished structures dating back to the 1800s, the Hotel Molina Lario is located centrally across from the Cathedral and conveniently near to the portside as well as the Picasso Museum.

All rooms include a mini-bar, a well-equipped bathroom, stereo sound system, hairdryer and free Internet. The decor is both modern and attractive.

The hotel has a swimming pool on the roof terrace that offers a great view of the city of Malaga and surroundings. Rooms have facilities for disabled guests and breakfast is included in the price. Accommodation begins at 110€.

Suite Novotel Malaga Centro

Calle San Jacinto 7, 29007 Malaga, Spain

http://www.suitenovotel.com/gb/booking/hotels-list.shtml

The decor of the Suite Novotel Malaga Centro is stylish

COSTA DEL SOL TRAVEL GUIDE

and modern and the hotel is just five minutes away from the center of Malagna. Each room offers adaptable, multi-functional furniture that can be transformed to serve a variety of needs. Rooms include television, entertainment in the form of large selection of music, game and video files as well as free Internet. The hotel has a fitness center as well.

Breakfast can be enjoyed in the designated area or in your room and there is also a self-service Boutique Gourmande for snacks. Accommodation begins at 79€. The hotel group belongs to a loyalty program that rewards repeat customers with benefits and discounts.

Hotel Isabelle, Torremolinos

Paseo Maritimo 47, Playamar, 29620 Torremolinos

http://www.hotelisabel.net/index

COSTA DEL SOL TRAVEL GUIDE

Hotel Isabelle offers spacious accommodation with great sea views. Rooms include satellite TV, air conditioning and Wi-Fi access. The decor style is attractive and friendly. The use of a safe or fridge can be arranged on request, but at an extra charge.

There are plenty of loungers at the hotel's swimming pool for sunbathing. Breakfast is included. Rooms begin at 99€.

Hotel Casa Rosa

Pensamiento n. 31, 29639 Benalmadena

http://www.hostalcasarosa.com/

Hotel Casa Rosa is a small, intimate hotel that offers excellent service and top-notch facilities despite its modest proportions. Rooms include satellite TV, a mini-bar, air-conditioning and Wi-Fi access. The village has plenty of character, and the breakfast buffet is recommended. Accommodation begins at 45€ a night.

La Villa Marbella

Calle Principe 10, Old Historic Town, 29600 Marbella, Spain

http://www.lavillamarbella.com/

You will find La Villa Marbella located centrally within the Old Town section of Marbella. The main building presents a beautifully harmonious picture with bougainvillea hugging its exterior and decorative stone detail marking the interior. It began as a cosy four-room establishment and now comprises 5 buildings and 21 rooms in total, each with its own individual charm and character.

The staff are attentive to the needs of guests. Rooms include free Internet and Wi-Fi access, satellite TV, air-conditioning and a mini-bar. Breakfast is included. Accommodation begins at 90€.

 Places to Eat

The Lounge at Pinoccios, Benalmadena

Avda Antonio Machado 57, Conjunto Las Gaviotas, 31-32, 29630 Benalmadena

Tel: 952 561 989

http://www.pinocciosbar.com/index.html

The Lounge at Pinoccios offers three separate menu options - light meals, tapas or dinner. The tapas menu includes a portion of crusty bread free of charge and

COSTA DEL SOL TRAVEL GUIDE

features dishes such as Thai fish cakes, Chicken wings, Chorizo in apple cider, nachos with melted cheese and salsa and asparagus rolled in ham.

The light meals menu offers a selection of toasted sandwiches, wraps, omelettes and baked potatoes. The dinner main menu includes items such as grilled chicken breast, Mediterranean cod and pork fillet with fresh apple in cider sauce.

The tapas portions range between 1.50€ and 3€ per item. For a light meal, expect to pay between 3€ and 6€ per item. Starters are priced between 2€ and 4.50€, whereas the mains are all priced under 15€.

COSTA DEL SOL TRAVEL GUIDE

Tapeo de Cervantes, Malaga

C/ Carcer, 8, 29012 Malaga, Spain

Tel: 952 609 458

http://www.eltapeodecervantes.com/

Tapeo de Cervantes is called the best tapas restaurant by some of its patrons. Some of the menu items include veal meatballs, ham flamenquines, fried squid wheels with lemon, chicken croquettes with peanut butter, sauteed pork, wild mushrooms and nuts, pumpkin and mushroom risotto, salmon and spinach scramble in raspberry vinegar and scampi with honey. Soak up the atmosphere of traditional Spanish dining. Meals range from 13.75€ to 20€.

COSTA DEL SOL TRAVEL GUIDE

Samsara Deli Café, Mijas

Calle Marbella, 5, 29649 La Cala de Mijas, Mijas

Tel: 952 494 816

Most dining in Spain relies heavily on meaty dishes. For a healthy alternative, visit Samsara Deli Cafe. While there are non-veggie choices such as chicken satay and meatballs, the vegetarian options take center stage.

A popular concept of this restaurant revolves around bamboo 'boats' filled with a variety of salad choices. Other items on the menu include smoothies and uniquely flavored ice creams. Expect to pay between 4€ and 12€.

El Gato Lounge, Torremolinos

Paseo Maritimo de Perdregal 1, 29620 Torremolinos

Tel: 687 871 165

http://elgatolounge.com/

The tables at El Gato Lounge extend towards the beachfront area for a scenic and relaxing experience. Menu items include a wide variety of creative salads, a number of toast options, baguettes, the tapas section and also a few combination boards to share.

Main menu items include dishes such as pork sirloin, chicken curry and meatballs with chorizo. The Tapas Experience includes four courses from a salad starter, to a selection of first cold tapas, then hot tapas and ending off with a dessert for 25€.

La Plaza, Malaga

Plaza de la Merced No.18, Malaga

Tel: 952 608 491

COSTA DEL SOL TRAVEL GUIDE

http://www.laplazamalaga.com/menu_en.html

If you visited Plaza de la Merced to view Picasso's birthplace and other sights of the historical district of Malaga, you may consider lingering in the area for a good meal.

As many eateries in the region, it offers a tapas option as well as a main menu. The restaurant also offers a variety of dessert options such as chocolate truffle tart with caramelized oranges, Beverages includes a selection of coffees, teas, smoothies, or cocktails. Some specialities include shrimp linguini, pumpkin risotto. Expect to pay between 35€ and 40€ for two.

COSTA DEL SOL TRAVEL GUIDE

🌍 Shopping

Artesania de Espana, Mijas

Calle Malaga, Mijas Pueblo

http://www.lionluis.com/Negocio/Ingles/artesania_ing.html

The market stalls and small shops in the town of Mijas offer a great selection of traditional handcrafted items. You will find a wonderful choice in ceramic items such as bowls, vases and plates. One of the best stops to make is at Artesania de Espana, a shop run by Luis Dominguez Calderon that provides an outlet for various artisans from the area. Items within the crowded shop are exquisitely made and elaborately decorated. Besides ceramics, he also stocks rosaries, jewellery, pewter items, Spanish fans, religious icons and even authentic army swords.

Costa del Sol Markets

http://www.sundream-estate.com/new-6-local-market-in-costa-del-sol.html

Most every town in Costa del Sol has a weekly market. While some have the character of a flea market or car boot sale, others offer a great opportunity to buy local crafts, or even items from locations such as Morocco or Thailand. The region is particularly reknowned for the quality of its ceramics and pottery.

Fuengirola has a Tuesday market that offers an abundance of fresh produce, and also crafts, especially houseware. The Saturday market in this town is more like a fleamarket, but you may stumble upon a geniune antique or some quality second hand goods.

COSTA DEL SOL TRAVEL GUIDE

Across from the bullring at Puerto Banus, a Saturday market trades in antiques, art, sculpture and functional art items. The Wednesday market at Avda. Juan Carlos in Estepona offers a large mix, including some great souvenirs. Marbella's weekly market is on Mondays at the fairground, while Malaga has a Sunday flea-market at the football stadium.

At Torremolinos the weekly market is on Thursdays at El Calvarío, while the Friday market at Benalmadena can be found near Tivoli World. Balcón de Europa at Nerja has a daily craft market every evening in the summer months.

Tickled Pink, Mijas Pueblo

For a huge selection of jewellery ranging from very cheap to expensive, visit this shop in Mijas. The items vary from

COSTA DEL SOL TRAVEL GUIDE

the delicate to more bulky costume pieces and include items that are worn for holistic rather than aesthetic reasons. They also sell ornaments, Swarovsky crystal pieces and Betty Boop memorabilia.

Old Town, Marbella

Despite a reputation for high fashion shops, Marbella also offers a great selection of ceramics, economic leather products and other local crafts in the old historical section, near to Plaza de las Naranjas (Orange Square).

Shopping Malls

There are malls in various regions of the Costa del Sol, often including childrens play areas. Parque Miramar in Avenida de la Encarnacion, Fuengirola has a large selection of fashion and convenience shops as well as restaurants to eat. In Malaga, you can choose between

COSTA DEL SOL TRAVEL GUIDE

the four-storey Larios Centro at 25 Avenida de la Aurora, the ultra-modern Malaga Plaza at 12 Calle Armengual de la Mota and the leisure paradise of Plaza Major at 1 Alfonso Ponce de Leon, Rotonda Parador de Golf. In Marbella, there are various malls to tempt you such as El Corte Ingles (the largest department store chain in Spain) at 2 Bulevar Principe Alfonso de Hohenioe and Plaza del Mar on Camilo Jose Cela.

Know Before You Go

 Entry Requirements

By virtue of the Schengen agreement, visitors from other countries in the European Union will not need a visa when visiting Spain. Additionally visitors from Switzerland, Norway, Lichtenstein, Iceland, Canada, the United Kingdom, Australia and the USA are also exempt. Independently travelling minors will need to carry written permission from their parents. If visiting from a country where you require a visa to enter Spain, you will also need to state the purpose of your visit and provide proof that you have financial means to support yourself for the duration of your stay. Unless you are an EU national, your passport should be valid for at least 3 months after the end of your stay.

Health Insurance

Citizens of other EU countries are covered for emergency health care in Spain. UK residents, as well as visitors from Switzerland are covered by the European Health Insurance Card (EHIC), which can be applied for free of charge. Visitors from non-Schengen countries will need to show proof of private health insurance that is valid for the duration of their stay in Spain, as part of their visa application.

🌐 Travelling with Pets

Spain participates in the Pet Travel Scheme (PETS) which allows UK residents to travel with their pets without requiring quarantine upon re-entry. Certain conditions will need to be met. The animal will have to be microchipped and up to date on rabies vaccinations. Additionally, you will need a PETS re-entry certificate issued by a UK vet, an Export Health Certificate (this is required by the Spanish authorities), an official Certificate of Treatment against dangerous parasites such as tapeworm and ticks and an official Declaration that your pet has not left the qualifying countries within this period. Pets from the USA or Canada may be brought in under the conditions of a non-commercial import. For this, your pet will also need to be microchipped (or marked with an identifying tattoo) and up to date on rabies vaccinations.

🌐 Airports

Adolfo Suárez Madrid–Barajas Airport (MAD) is the largest and busiest airport in Spain. It is located about 9km from the financial district of Madrid, the capital. The busiest route is the

COSTA DEL SOL TRAVEL GUIDE

so-called "Puente Aéreo" or "air bridge", which connects Madrid with Barcelona. The second busiest airport in Spain is **Barcelona–El Prat Airport** (BCN), located about 14km southwest from the center of Barcelona. There are two terminals. The newer Terminal 1 handles the bulk of its traffic, while the older Terminal 2 is used by budget airlines such as EasyJet.

Palma de Mallorca Airport (PMI) is the third largest airport in Spain and one of its busiest in the summer time. It has the capacity of processing 25 million passengers annually. **Gran Canaria Airport** (LPA) handles around 10 million passengers annually and connects travellers with the Canary Islands. **Pablo Ruiz Picasso Malaga Airport** (AGP) provides access to the Costa del Sol. Other southern airports are **Seville Airport** (SVQ), **Jaen Federico Garcia Lorca Airport** (GRX) near Granada, **Jerez de la Frontera Airport**, which connects travellers to Costa del Luz and Cadiz and **Almeria Airport** (LEI).

Airlines

Iberia is the flag carrying national airline of Spain. Since a merger in 2010 with British Airways, it is part of the International Airlines Group (IAG). Iberia is in partnership with the regional carrier Air Nostrum and Iberia Express, which focusses on medium and short haul routes. Vueling is a low-

COSTA DEL SOL TRAVEL GUIDE

cost Spanish airline with connections to over 100 destinations. In partnership with MTV, it also provides a seasonal connection to Ibiza. Volotea is a budget airline based in Barcelona, which mainly flies to European destinations. Air Europe, the third largest airline after Iberia and Vueling connects Europe to resorts in the Canaries and the Balearic Islands and also flies to North and South America. Swiftair flies mainly to destinations in Europe, North Africa and the Middle East.

Barcelona-El Prat Airport serves as a primary hub for Iberia Regional. It is also a hub for Vueling. Additionally it functions as a regional hub for Ryanair. Air Europe's primary hubs are at Palma de Mallorca Airport and Madrid Barajas Airport, but other bases are at Barcelona Airport and Tenerife South Airport. Air Nostrum is served by hubs at Barcelona Airport, Madrid Barajas Airport and Valencia Airport. Gran Canaria Airport is the hub for the regional airline, Binter Canarias.

🌍 Currency

Spain's currency is the Euro. It is issued in notes in denominations of €500, €200, €100, €50, €20, €10 and €5. Coins are issued in denominations of €2, €1, 50c, 20c, 10c, 5c, 2c and 1c.

COSTA DEL SOL TRAVEL GUIDE

🌐 Banking & ATMs

You should have no trouble making withdrawals in Spain if your ATM card is compatible with the MasterCard/Cirrus or Visa/Plus networks. If you want to save money, avoid using the dynamic currency conversion (DCC) system, which promises to charge you in your own currency for the Euros you withdraw. The fine print is that your rate will be less favorable. Whenever possible, opt to conduct your transaction in Euros instead. Do remember to advise your bank or credit card company of your travel plans before leaving.

🌐 Credit Cards

Visa and MasterCard will be accepted at most outlets that handle credit cards in Spain, but you may find that your American Express card is not as welcome at all establishments. While shops may still be able to accept transactions with older magnetic strip cards, you will need a PIN enabled card for transactions at automatic vendors such as ticket sellers. Do not be offended when asked to show proof of ID when paying by credit card. It is common practice in Spain and Spaniards are required by law to carry identification on them at all times.

🌐 Tourist Taxes

In the region of Catalonia, which includes Barcelona, a tourist tax of between €0.45 and €2.50 per night is levied for the first seven days of your stay. The amount depends on the standard of the establishment, but includes youth hostels, campgrounds, holiday apartments and cruise ships with a stay that exceeds 12 hours.

🌐 Reclaiming VAT

If you are not from the European Union, you can claim back VAT (or Value Added Tax) paid on your purchases in Spain. The VAT rate in Spain is 18 percent. VAT refunds are made on purchases of €90.15 and over from a single shop. Look for shops displaying Global Blue Tax Free Shopping signage. You will be required to fill in a form at the shop, which must then be stamped at the Customs office at the airport. Customs officers will want to inspect your purchases to make sure that they are sealed and unused. Once this is done, you will be able to claim your refund from the Refund Office at the airport. Alternately, you can mail the form to Global Blue once you get home for a refund on your credit card.

COSTA DEL SOL TRAVEL GUIDE

🌐 Tipping policy

In general, Spain does not really have much of a tipping culture and the Spanish are not huge tippers themselves. When in a restaurant, check your bill to see whether a gratuity is already included. If not, the acceptable amount will depend on the size of the meal, the prestige of the restaurant and the time of day. For a quick coffee, you can simply round the amount off. For lunch in a modest establishment, opt for 5 percent or one euro per person. The recommended tip for dinner would be more generous, usually somewhere between 7 and 10 percent. This will depend on the type of establishment.

In hotels, if there is someone to help you with your luggage, a tip of 1 euro should be sufficient. At railway stations and airports, a tip is not really expected. Rounding off the amount of the fare to the nearest euro would be sufficient for a taxi driver. If you recruited a private driver, you may wish to tip that person at the end of your association with him.

🌐 Mobile Phones

Most EU countries, including Spain uses the GSM mobile service. This means that most UK phones and some US and Canadian phones and mobile devices will work in Spain. While you could check with your service provider about coverage before you leave, using your own service in roaming mode will involve additional costs. The alternative is to purchase a Spanish SIM card to use during your stay in Spain.

Spain has four mobile networks. They are Movistar, Vodafone, Orange and Yoiga. Buying a Spanish SIM card is relatively simple and inexpensive. By law, you will be required to show some form of identification such as a passport. A basic SIM card from Vodafone costs €5. There are two tourist packages available for €15, which offers a combination of 1Gb data, together with local and international call time. Alternately, a data only package can also be bought for €15. From Orange, you can get a SIM card for free, with a minimum top-up purchase of €10. A tourist SIM with a combination of data and voice calls can be bought for €15. Movistar offers a start-up deal of €10. At their sub-branches, Tuenti, you can also get a free SIM, but the catch is that you need to choose a package to get it. The start-up cost at Yoiga is €20.

🌐 Dialling Code

The international dialling code for Spain is +34.

🌐 Emergency Numbers

All Emergencies: 112 (no area code required)
Police (municipal): 092
Police (national): 091

COSTA DEL SOL TRAVEL GUIDE

Police (tourist police, Madrid): 91 548 85 37

Police (tourist police, Barcelona): 93 290 33 27

Ambulance: 061 or 112

Fire: 080 or 112

Traffic: 900 123 505

Electricity: 900 248 248

Immigration: 900 150 000

MasterCard: 900 958 973

Visa: 900 99 1124

Public Holidays

1 January: New Year's Day (Año Nuevo)

6 January: Day of the Epiphany/Three Kings Day (Reyes Mago)

March/April: Good Friday

1 May: Labor Day (Día del Trabajo)

15 August: Assumption of Mary (Asunción de la Virgen)

12 October: National Day of Spain/Columbus Day (Fiesta Nacional de España or Día de la Hispanidad)

1 November: All Saints Day (Fiesta de Todos los Santos)

6 December: Spanish Constitution Day (Día de la Constitución)

8 December: Immaculate Conception (La Immaculada)

25 December: Christmas (Navidad)

Easter Monday is celebrated in the Basque region, Castile-La Mancha, Catalonia, La Rioja, Navarra and Valencia. 26

COSTA DEL SOL TRAVEL GUIDE

December is celebrated as Saint Stephen's Day in Catalonia and the Balearic Islands.

Time Zone

Spain falls in the Central European Time Zone. This can be calculated as Greenwich Mean Time/Co-ordinated Universal Time (GMT/UTC) +2; Eastern Standard Time (North America) -6; Pacific Standard Time (North America) -9.

Daylight Savings Time

Clocks are set forward one hour on the last Sunday in March and set back one hour on the last Sunday in October for Daylight Savings Time.

School Holidays

Spain's academic year is from mid-September to mid-June. It is divided into three terms with two short breaks of about two weeks around Christmas and Easter.

Trading Hours

Trading hours in Spain usually run from 9.30am to 1.30pm and from 4.30pm to 8pm, from Mondays to Saturdays. Malls and shopping centers often trade from 10am to 9pm without closing. During the peak holiday seasons, shops could stay open until 10pm. Lunch is usually served between 1pm and 3.30pm while dinner is served from 8.30 to 11pm.

🌐 Driving Laws

The Spanish drive on the right hand side of the road. You will need a driver's licence which is valid in the EC to be able to hire a car in Spain. The legal driving age is 18, but most rental companies will require you to be at least 21 to be able to rent a car. You will need to carry your insurance documentation and rental contract with you at all times, when driving. The speed limit in Spain is 120km per hour on motorways, 100km per hour on dual carriageways and 90km per hour on single carriageways. Bear in mind that it is illegal to drive in Spain wearing sandals or flip-flops.

You may drive a non-Spanish vehicle in Spain provided that it is considered roadworthy in the country where it is registered. As a UK resident, you will be able to drive a vehicle registered in the UK in Spain for up to six months, provided that your liabilities as a UK motorist, such as MOT, road tax and insurance are up to date for the entire period of your stay. The legal limit in Spain is 0.05, but for new drivers who have had their licence for less than two years, it is 0.03.

🌐 Drinking Laws

In Spain, the minimum drinking age is 18. Drinking in public places is forbidden and can be punished with a spot fine. In areas where binge drinking can be a problem, alcohol trading hours are often limited.

🌐 Smoking Laws

In the beginning of 2006, Spain implemented a policy banning smoking from all public and private work places. This includes schools, libraries, museums, stadiums, hospitals, cinemas, theatres and shopping centers as well as public transport. From 2011, smoking was also banned in restaurants and bars, although designated smoking areas can be created provided they are enclosed and well ventilated. Additionally tobacco products may only be sold from tobacconists and bars and restaurants where smoking is permitted. Smoking near children's parks, schools or health centers carries a €600 fine.

🌐 Electricity

Electricity: 220 volts
Frequency: 50 Hz
Your electrical appliances from the UK and Ireland should be able to function sufficiently in Spain, but since Spain uses 2 pin

COSTA DEL SOL TRAVEL GUIDE

sockets, you will need a C/F adapter to convert the plug from 3 to 2-pins. The voltage and frequency is compatible with UK appliances. If travelling from the USA, you will need a converter or step-down transformer to convert your appliances to 110 volts. The latest models of many laptops, camcorders, cell phones and digital cameras are dual-voltage with a built in converter.

🌐 Food & Drink

Spanish cuisine is heavily influenced by a Moorish past. Staple dishes include the rice dish, Paella, Jamon Serrano (or Spanish ham), Gazpacho (cold tomato-based vegetable soup), roast suckling pig, chorizo (spicy sausage) and the Spanish omelette. Tapas (hot or cold snacks) are served with drinks in Spanish bars.

The most quintessentially Spanish drink is sangria, but a popular alternative with the locals is tinto de verano, or summer wine, a mix of red wine and lemonade. Vino Tinto or red wine compliments most meal choices. The preferred red grape type is Tempranillo, for which the regions of Roija and Ribera del Duero are famous. A well-known sparkling wine, Cava, is grown in Catalonia. Do try the Rebujito, a Seville style mix of sherry, sparkling water and mint. The most popular local beers are Cruzcampo, Alhambra and Estrello Damm. Coffee is also popular with Spaniards, who prefer Café con leche (espresso with milk).

Websites

http://www.idealspain.com

A detailed resource that includes legal information for anyone planning a longer stay or residency in Spain.

http://spainattractions.es/

http://www.tourspain.org/

http://spainguides.com/

http://www.travelinginspain.com/

http://wikitravel.org/en/Spain

Printed in Great Britain
by Amazon